The story of
Hook Norton

for readers of all ages

Sean Callery
Hook Norton Local History Group

Contents

Hook Norton, also known as Hooky, has a long history that includes:

- Ovens bigger than houses
- Speeding steam trains
- A Viking massacre
- Bossy kings
- A famous brewery
- Helping 'mad' people
- Armies heading for battle

… but you'll have to read on to get the story in the right order!

Two towers

Look at Hooky from the hills around it, and the towers of the church and the brewery stand out. St Peter's has been at the centre of village life for centuries, as a place of worship, a store for legal papers and fire-fighting equipment, and as a stronghold. The brewery is known around the world, and attracts visitors keen to take a guided tour and see a building and machinery that have hardly changed in more than 100 years.

Different landscape

By the early 1900s the view of Hooky was dominated by the huge viaducts that stretched across one side of the village, and the plumes of dust, smoke and steam that rose from quarries, ironworks and the trains that hauled away valuable cargo.

Here in Hooky…

No one is sure how Scotland End, on Hooky's west side, got its name. It could be from 'scot', an old word for a special tax.

Hooky's 3 Bs

Hooky was once a typical rural community where the key things in life were the 3 Bs:

- Beer: weaker than today's drink, and safer than water.
- Bread: the main food in everyday diet, often made at home.
- Bacon: meat from the family's pigs. As villagers once said: 'The only thing you can't eat is the squeal!'

Horse power

For centuries, it wasn't unusual to walk to nearby towns such as Chipping Norton to work or see family. Some villagers rarely left Hooky, and those who did often went by horse and cart.

Rising totals

Hooky's population rose slowly for centuries until a recent rapid increase:

1086	400
1676	600
1801	1,032
1901	1,386
1971	1,361
2011	2,596

The massive rise in population for 2011 is partly due to the many new houses that were built. But the total now also includes two smaller nearby villages.

◀ Old cottages have often seen many changes. A small window high on an end wall is often a sign that there was once a bedroom just under the roof before the thatch was replaced by tiles.

Changing village

In the 19th century Hooky changed from leafy countryside to a dirty, noisy industrial landscape. Since then, it has evolved again as the quarries closed, the railway line shut, and housing estates have gone up. Now most people drive to work, and big concerns are things like broadband speed and our carbon footprint.

Ticket to history

This book takes you on a ride through the history of Hooky – and along the way, look out for the train ticket symbol like the one opposite to find out some surprising facts.

Hooky was a seabed and then a land of dinosaurs before becoming home to a small settlement near a path trekked by travellers for thousands of years.

Hooky-by-the-sea

You can tell Hooky was once under water from the tiny seashells in the local stone. Millions of years ago, the bodies of these creatures were crushed into layers of rock. Some layers also held iron ore that was later dug up (see pages 30–31).

Hooky is built on seaside rock!

The Rollright Stones is an ancient ceremonial site.

Dinosaur land

Dinosaurs once roamed Hooky. The fossil of one has been found on a local farm. It was as long as a bus and had metre-long spikes to protect its body from sharp-toothed predators while it browsed for plants to munch. Lexovisaurus died out when dry weather killed its food supply.

Lexovisaurus lived about 160 million years ago.

Many sites

Before Hook Norton was built, the area was home to many people. This table shows the ancient sites we know of within 6 miles of St Peter's:

Bronze Age sites	28
Iron Age sites	75
Roman sites	145
Other ancient sites	26

The Jurassic Way

Travellers and farmers made the first trackways on high ground that was neither soggy nor hard to cross. One just north of the village, sometimes called The Jurassic Way, leads past the Rollright Stones 4 miles west. This area was used for burials for at least 5,000 years, and includes the 'King's Men': 77 rocks carefully laid in a mysterious circle, probably for ancient ceremonies.

Hillfort

East along the track is the site of Tadmarton hillfort, built between 1000 and 800 BC. It was about 165 metres across and protected by 1.8-metre high earth walls.

TADMARTON 3

**WIGGINTON ½
CHIPPING NORTON 7**

Before Hooky existed, there was a hillfort at Tadmarton and a Roman villa in Wigginton.

Here in Hooky...

There was another camp that is now visible only from the air about a mile west of the one at Tadmarton Heath. Nothing remains except the name: Campfield.

Roman remains

After the Romans conquered southern Britain from 43 AD on, they let the local tribes continue to rule. There was a Roman villa in Wigginton, a couple of miles to the east. Also, Roman coins and a brooch have been dug up in Hook Norton. The brooch is now in Oxford's Ashmolean Museum.

◀ This drawing shows a mosaic in the Roman villa in nearby Wigginton.

On the frontier

Hook Norton sat on the border between rival Saxon kingdoms … until in 913 some even more dangerous warriors came.

Royal village on a border

Here in Hooky…

A burial site with two Viking skeletons and 23 Saxon coins was found in Hook Norton in 1848.

Saxon settlers crossed from mainland Europe in the fifth century and built small villages of wooden thatched houses near where they grazed their pigs, cattle and sheep. Hook Norton was one such settlement. It stood on the frontier between the kingdoms of Wessex and Mercia, which were sometimes enemies and sometimes friends. An early document lists Hook Norton as a 'royal vill', meaning the village was owned by the king.

Why Hook Norton?

'Hook Norton' comes from the Anglo-Saxon for 'settlement on the hill slope of Hocca's people'. Hocca was probably a Saxon nobleman. Some historians believe that the village was first built near the Jurassic Way, close to the hillfort (see page 7), and moved to its present site sometime after the battle of 913.

Many names

Documents give many different names for the village over the years.

913	Hocneratune
1050	Hocceneretune
1086	Hochenartone
1129	Hokenorton
1216	Hogenarton
1251	Hogenorthon and Hogenortone
1263	Okenardton
1316	Hoggenorton
1346	Hognorton
1430	Hegnorton
1535	Hokenorton
1655	Hooking Norton and Hookin Norton

The Danes are coming!

New invaders attacked England. We call them Vikings, but they were known as Danes. They began by landing along the east coast, and these fierce fighters later marched inland and turned Northampton, 40 miles away, into a stronghold. From here they raided Saxon kingdoms.

Many locals died in a terrible battle near Tadmarton hillfort in 913. Maybe the surviving Saxons fled from their wrecked wooden houses, and later built a new village a short distance to the southwest. We know that the settlement of Hook Norton existed where it now is from some time after this date.

After Easter an army of the Pagans from Northampton and from Leicester plundered in the county of Oxenford, and slew a great number of persons in the royal town of Hokenertune.

John of Worcester, a historian monk, writing later about the battle of 913.

The first church

Archaeologists say now-hidden parts of St Peter's are Anglo-Saxon, probably late in the 10th century.

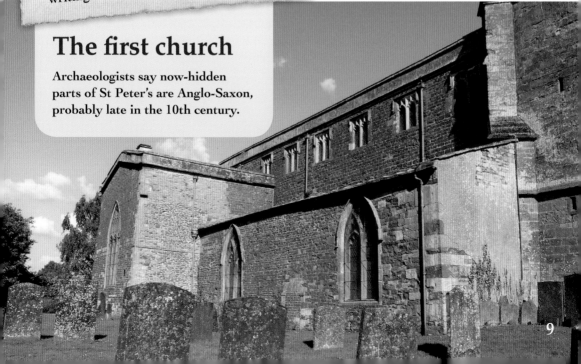

9

The £30 village

Hook Norton became a royal present after William of Normandy defeated Harold II at the Battle of Hastings in 1066.

William wins
The Bayeux tapestry tells the story of the Norman invasion of England.

Royal spoils

William the Conqueror allowed Wigod, a Saxon nobleman who had helped him, to keep possession of Hook Norton. William also gave many Oxfordshire lands to his Norman supporter, Robert d'Oily, who married Wigod's daughter Ealdgyth. So when Wigod died, Robert d'Oily became Baron Hook Norton. The d'Oily family had a big say in how the village was run for the next 180 years.

Valuable village

In 1086 William's officials began the Domesday Book, a list of all the buildings and land in England that could be taxed. The entry for Hook Norton said it was worth £30 a year. In this table, 'Households' counts the number of men who headed families and if we guess the women and children, we can say that Hooky's population was about 400. So at that time it was larger and more valuable than Chipping Norton, but not some other villages.

Village	Value in 1086	Households
Banbury	£44	135
Bloxham	£67	115
Chipping Norton	£22	53
Hook Norton	£30	84

The Hook Norton entry in the Domesday Book. ▶

St Peter's grows

Norman churches were used for worship and also as safe places to protect people and valuables. Robert d'Oily increased the size of the existing Saxon church, choosing a typical Norman design: a large building in the shape of a cross.

The font in St Peter's church is from Norman times, although some of the carvings were added later. The images include Adam and Eve near the Tree of Knowledge in a scene from the Bible.

Colourful images of St Peter and St Paul were added around 1400. They were then painted over but some have since been uncovered.

Here in Hooky…

In around 1200, one person chose to be walled up inside the church to spend their life in prayer and worship.

Shared out

The second Robert d'Oily set up Oseney Abbey near Oxford in 1129 and his family continued to help the Abbey for over 100 years. Their gifts included part of Hook Norton. Now Hooky was made up of two 'manors': one belonging to a powerful family, the other to a monastery.

Workers had to give some of their crops to the d'Oilys and Oseney Abbey to pay for using the land.

Strips of land

SOUTHROP ROAD

On the other side of the stream that runs through Hook Norton was the settlement of Southrop, first mentioned in 1316. Its name means 'South town'.

Several rich families controlled much of Hooky through medieval times. Hooky's villagers had to work in the owner's lands for the right to farm the surrounding fields.

Ruling family

The title 'Baron Hook Norton' passed down the d'Oily family. Each time they had to pay the King a fee. For example, in 1229 Thomas d'Oily handed over £100 (a fortune to most people then) and two horses. The title later went to his sister, Margery, who married into the de Plesset family – and they took over the title after her death in 1253, but soon lost it because of money problems. One of the de Plesset wives, called Isabel, is buried in St Peter's church.

Children on the land

In medieval times, the lord or the church did not actually own land: instead, the king allowed them to use it. In the open field system, land around Hooky was split into narrow strips and shared out among villagers. Children worked with their parents on this land, took cattle to graze on shared common land – where they might also collect wood for the fire – and helped to look after the family's pig, cow or chickens.

We can still see the ridges that show how fields were once divided into strips.

Adding the tower was a big, expensive job.

The church grows

The biggest change to St Peter's in medieval times was building the tower in the 15th century. Church bells could now be rung to call villagers together. Also, the walls were raised and painted, and parts of the building were widened. The new roof beams were supported by carved stones called corbels. These often show funny or scary faces.

Stone corbels were added to ▲ hold up the raised roof. They were carved to look like faces or animals.

Here in Hooky...

In 1414 the manor of Hook Norton passed to Thomas Chaucer, son of writer Geoffrey Chaucer, famous for his poem 'The Canterbury Tales'.

Water spout
Gargoyles often decorated gutters that let water off the roof.

13

Keep your head

PARK ROAD

This leads to The Park (now Park Farm), which was a Tudor term for a deer park.

Henry VIII, Anne Boleyn, the Mary Rose: all these Tudor icons had links to Hook Norton.

Heading off

Some people challenged the right of the Tudors to rule. One was Edmund de la Pole, who was already Duke of Suffolk and lord of Hook Norton – but he wanted to be king. In 1513 Henry VIII ended the argument by chopping Edmund's head off! Now Henry could say who would run Hook Norton.

Old pals

Henry chose Charles Brandon, who had spent many nights partying with the King, and was rewarded in 1514 with titles and possessions, including the manor of Hook Norton. But a year later Brandon annoyed his important and impatient friend by not asking permission before he married the King's sister Mary – after whom the famous ship was later named. Henry was furious, but did nothing … for now.

▲ A wedding portrait of Charles Brandon and Mary.

Royal visit

After Mary died in 1533, Henry demanded that Brandon pay back money he owed. Brandon claimed he was short of cash because he had spent £1,500 on improving the deer hunt in Hook Norton. A suspicious Henry VIII came to see Hooky for himself with his queen, Anne Boleyn, and was very grumpy about the lack of deer and the poor condition of the hunting lodge. But Brandon escaped the axe once again.

Henry VIII at about the time he visited Hooky in 1535. ▶

The Garrett House

Charles Brandon did more for the villagers than many previous rulers. In 1522 he handed over a house and garden in the High Street, called The Garrett House, 'to the use and common advantage' of the poor, giving shelter to homeless families. Next-door houses were added, and this help continued until the 1770s. The charity still handed out money until the 20th century.

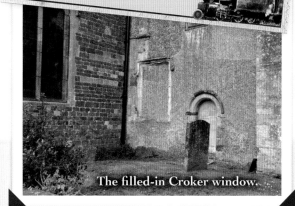

Here in Hooky...

Rent for the old abbey lands went to the Bishop of Oxford, but Queen Elizabeth I didn't make anyone bishop for decades – so the money went to her instead!

The filled-in Croker window.

Farewell Oseney, hello Crokers

Henry VIII's battle with the Catholic Church and its leader, the Pope, ended with him setting up his own Church of England in 1534, and seizing church-controlled lands. These included the parts of Hook Norton run by Oseney Abbey, broken up in 1539. A rich local man called John Croker took over the lands and his family was in charge of much of the village for the next 100 years.

Many of the family are buried in St Peter's, and John is remembered by a memorial stone called the Croker Stone, dated 1568, in the north aisle. But this is not the only memory of the family at St Peter's: the Crokers were so powerful they even had their own window put in so they could see their prayer books more easily. It was filled in later, but you can see its shape (above) on the outside of the south wall.

Pray stay!

In the 17th century Hook Norton welcomed new religious faiths – and an army fighting the King.

Hooky in the Civil War

King Charles I fell out with Parliament over taxes and religion in the mid-17th century, and went to war. Armies criss-crossed the country, and on 2 September 1643, 5,000 Roundheads camped for the night in Hooky. These soldiers were against the King, and many wanted to change how the country worshipped.

Church protest

Those most unhappy with the Church of England became Baptists and Quakers. These groups soon gained followers and would later build churches in Hook Norton.

Here in Hooky...
After 400 years' absence from Hooky, a Roman Catholic church opened in 1932, closing in 1997.

CHAPEL STREET

Chapel Street is named after the Methodist chapel built in that part of the High Street in 1875. It was demolished in 1986.

Pestered pastor

These 'nonconformists' soon met trouble in Hook Norton. During the 1660s soldiers broke up a Baptist service and put pastors James Wilmot and Charles Archer in Oxford jail. Wilmot later got a £20 fine (worth several thousand pounds today) and all his furniture was seized when he didn't pay. But his grateful supporters bought it back.

New Protestant faiths

1644	1668	1718	1794
Baptists start worshipping in Hook Norton.	Quaker preachers visit and, in 1704, a group builds a meeting house in Southrop.	The first Baptist chapel goes up on Netting Street and is re-built in 1787 – it's still there today.	Methodists meet in a private house, and later build a chapel in Down End where the cemetery is now.

A Baptist Church

Local landowner and Baptist supporter William Harwood gave the group land for a chapel on Netting Street in 1718. He was among the first to be buried in its graveyard, in 1720. The chapel was re-built in 1787 and still stands – with a stone bearing Harwood's initials.

Church count

More new churches were founded from the 1790s, starting with the Methodists, who 50 years later themselves saw a breakaway move by poorer people. Local churches counted worshippers at their services in March 1851. The results show that over half of Hooky's 1,500 villagers went to church.

Church of England (St Peter's)	375
Methodists	174
Baptists	140
Primitive Methodists	100
Quakers	11

Some nonconformists banned music in their services, but the Wesleyans loved it and had their own band. ▷

1845	1873	1875	1898
A new group called the Primitive Methodists is active in the village.	The Baptists build a Sunday School room near their chapel.	A new Methodist chapel is built on what becomes known as Chapel Street.	Zion Chapel is built where East End meets Tite Lane, for the Strict Baptists.

A divided village

EAST END

East End once led to Workhouse Lane, so called because the village poor house was there from 1774 to 1835.

Some Hooky villagers got rich in the 17th and 18th centuries, but life got harder for others. The gap between them widened as farms replaced land strips.

Space saver

Lots of stone houses were built in Hooky between 1650 and 1720, showing that some people were becoming better off. A few of the new buildings had semi-circular outer walls to allow room for a curved staircase.

Farms are born

For centuries, villagers (known as commoners) had grown crops on strips of open land and grazed their animals on shared common land. This changed with the Enclosure Act of 1774. Now scattered strips were replaced by farms that were marked out by hedges. Richer owners now bought out poorer people, who became landless labourers.

Help from the grave

As the number of poor grew, some people left money to the poor in their wills. An inscription in St Peter's remembers William Hobbs, who in 1810:

... gave to the Minister and Churchwardens £5... for the Education of Poor Boys on ye Sabbath Day.

Hedges for edges

There were almost no hedges around Hooky before enclosure. Those planted at that time still mark out some fields today.

Little earners

Children earned money by killing creatures that ate the precious crops in the fields. These included:

> **Sparrows:** 2d per dozen
>
> **Foxes:** 2 shillings each
>
> **Hedgehogs** (or 'urchins'): 4d each
>
> **Woodpeckers** (or 'hickwals'): 4d each

Children would take bags with proof of their catch (such as birds' heads or foxes' feet) to the churchwarden at St Peter's, who then paid them from village funds. 2d was two old pennies. 12d made a shilling, which is now 5p.

Madhouses

Hooky had its own private asylum for people with mental health problems – its main building on Brick Hill is now called Bridge House. The owners later opened a second madhouse. The patients mainly came from outside the village.

Bridge House was once part of an asylum. ▼

Here in Hooky…

Each parish had to help its own poor. Eleven families were forced to leave in 1771 because the village would not support them.

Mad times

1725

The asylum is treating patients by now.

1775

Licence laws show that it is still the only asylum in Oxfordshire.

1817

Its patient numbers double to 20, and rise to 30 by 1835.

1835

The owner builds a second asylum in Down End. It has up to 90 patients – mostly very poor – housed behind a 4-metre high wall. The land the Down End asylum men farm close by is known as 'Madman's Yard'.

1842

The Bridge House asylum now takes only male patients.

1845

Oxfordshire builds its own asylums and poor patients are soon removed from Hooky.

1850

Bridge House now has only two patients, though there are still 50 in Down End.

1854

The owner closes both asylums.

19

Early schools

Education became more valued from the 19th century, but many families needed their children to earn, not learn.

A new school

At the school built in 1855, girls and boys used different entrances and playgrounds. The schoolmaster lived in the house built right next door.

No school ... again

Many parents kept their children away from school at times. Boys worked on the land, girls had to knit, sew and make bonnets and lace. The school shut in late summer for the harvest – but in October 1875 the headmaster complained that pupils were absent for 'apple picking, potato gathering, acorn collecting and many more [jobs]'.

▲ A Hooky class from the 1910s.

Learn to work

Children learned to read and write using chalk and slate. In 1875, when a new subject was added, the school log book says:

Mrs W came to complain about her grandson having to learn Geography or 'Grogery' as she termed it. She said: 'it was only fit for Gentlefolks and not for lads who would soon have to follow the plough tail'.

Annie Cross, a pupil (from 1909) and then teacher, said many lessons taught work skills: 'The girls knitted and did needlework. The boys were taught gardening.'

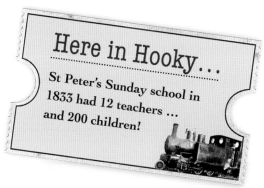

Dame schools

Some richer families who didn't need their children to work from an early age sent them to schools in local houses, called Dame schools because they were run by women. There were several on the High Street (see one below) and one each on Sibford Road and Down End.

A busy class in what is now the library.

First schools

1762

Charity School starts at St Peter's church.

1842

A nonconformist British School opens, until 1870.

1855

The 'National School' (run by the church) is built next to St Peter's. It's now the library.

1880

Law passed saying every child aged 5–10 years must go to school. Parents had to pay a penny a week for this.

1893

School-leaving age is raised to 11, and six years later to 12.

1900

Infant school opens for younger children on the same site.

1918

School-leaving age raised to 14, and schooling becomes free.

DOWN END

There was a Dame School here in 1829.

21

Hard times

In the 19th century everyone in the family helped to put food on the table.

QUEEN STREET

Queen Street was called Garrett Lane until Queen Victoria's Diamond Jubilee in 1897.

Shopping street

Visitors would walk or ride by horse from nearby villages to tour the many shops in Hooky. Most are now homes, but you can sometimes spot their previous uses by house names like 'The Old Sweet Shop'. Another clue is if they have large front windows, needed to display shop goods and let in lots of light.

Different jobs

Many villagers worked on the land, but some of the other jobs shown in the census of 1871 show how different life was compared with now. It listed 133 craftsmen and tradesmen in the village. Many people did more than one kind of work: for example, about ten years later, we know that when Austin Hall wasn't serving drinks at the Sun Inn, he made coffins! Typical jobs at the time are shown on the right.

Blacksmith: made iron tools, and fitted horse shoes.

Coal dealer: sold the key fuel of the time.

Cooper: made barrels, which were vital containers.

Hawker: sold objects door to door, as most people couldn't travel far to shop.

Laundress: had a supply of hot water for washing clothes.

Saddler: made leather equipment for working with animals.

Thatcher: fitted straw roofing.

Wheelwright: made and fixed wheels for carts needed for transport.

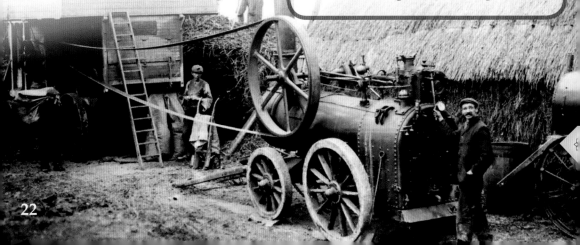

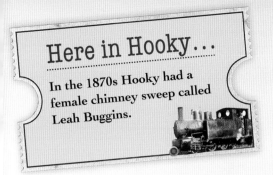

All the family worked in the fields at harvest time.

Kid power

Children worked on the land, fetching and carrying, or scaring birds off the crops. From the age of nine, ploughboys would lead the ox or horse that pulled ploughs to dig the soil. Children often learned their parents' trade, and from their 15th birthday they could be apprentices and learn a job. In these days before cars, the horse and cart was the best way to travel, and children in Hooky were as used to horses as they are today to computers.

Women's work

Women had many jobs, including making clothes, gloves and hats, working as cleaners and helping run the family business – some also brewed beer.

Hook Norton St Peters Day Festival

The rise of the machines

Machines were invented to help farmers, meaning there was less work for labourers. This picture shows the kind of equipment introduced in the 19th century, although it was taken later.

◀ St Peter's Day tea parties were held at the end of June from 1891 in the garden of the rectory at the top of Down End. Everyone dressed in their best clothes and sat at tables to tuck into sandwiches and treats.

An industrial landscape

This long, straight road was used for twisting cord into rope – vital for building work.

From late in the 19th century, Hooky's fields turned from green to grey as quarries replaced farms.

Smoke drifts from the ironworks over Hooky's two railway viaducts and blows on towards the centre of the village.

Big task

Hooky's local stone contained iron that could be melted to make steel. The only way to get this valuable ore from Hook Norton to the faraway steelworks was by train – so a railway was needed. Tunnels were burrowed, and 13 stone pillars up to 26 metres high were built to get the track across two valleys. Later, huge kilns blazed to burn the rock and release its ore – blasting clouds of steam and stinking gas into the skies over Hooky.

The 13 pillars

The viaduct pillars became known as 'the pyramids of Oxfordshire', comparing their gigantic size and the effort to build them with the famous ancient Egyptian tombs.

Line plan

By the 1860s short stretches of line had been built from Chipping Norton to Cheltenham. The extension to Banbury was planned to go through Swerford or Sibford, but the route was changed to come via Hook Norton, even though this was more difficult.

Work started in 1876 but was interrupted by cost problems. So the tunnels were narrowed from double track width to one track wide to save money.

Here in Hooky...

30-metre long iron girders bridged the gaps between the stone towers.

Industry arrives

1845

Work begins on parts of a railway between Chipping Norton and Cheltenham.

1874

The suggested train route is changed so that the line goes past Hook Norton's iron ore quarries.

1876

2,000 men with 120 horses begin digging out tunnels and a cutting between Chipping Norton and Hooky.

1883

400 men start work on the viaducts.

1887

The first train runs along the whole line.

1889

Large-scale quarrying begins.

Hands on

Getting the railway line to Hooky was a massive and dangerous job, carried out by an army of workers using shovels, picks and wheelbarrows.

A train steams along the cutting just after the Hook Norton tunnel.

Digging deep

It took seven years to finish the cutting and two tunnels. The cutting (which is when earth is removed so that the track runs through a hill) was up to 23 metres deep, and about 200,000 tons of rock and soil were carted away and piled up to create an embankment, or mound, between the two viaducts. Two men died working on the cutting. The tunnel closest to Hooky stretched for 382 metres. Today it's bricked up, but the constant sound of dripping water from inside shows how difficult it must have been to keep dry.

Rising high

Two viaducts were needed, with five and eight solid stone towers (called piers), each up to 26 metres high – and there are about 2,000 stone blocks in one tower alone. Workers perched on wooden scaffolding to fix them in place. In December 1885 Charles Hicks and Edward Gaskins fell to their deaths when the scaffolding collapsed.

▲ Wooden cranes lifted the stone blocks into place.

Navvies take a break on the cutting that they dug.

Here in Hooky...

Police broke up a massive fight in 1883 after a manager stole the navvies' pay.

Navvies

The workmen were known as 'navvies' after the labourers who dug the 'navigation canals' in the previous century. They lived in huts near the railway line, paying extra to sleep in a bed rather than on the floor. Their families came too – so their children went to school. The headmaster complained about their behaviour in the 1886 school diary (see right).

Some of the children belonging to the navvies who are at work in the parish are addicted to swearing ... If we could legally do so, I would rather be without any of them.

This photograph shows how the completed viaducts with their railway track could be seen for miles around the village.

27

On track

THE SIDINGS

The Sidings is near where there were once extra railway tracks for loading goods onto wagons.

Hooky's railway line was built to carry ironstone, but passengers could ride to Britain's west or east coasts on it.

Where shall we go?

From 1906 Hook Norton was on the 'coast-to-coast' route that linked Newcastle in northeast England with Swansea in Wales – although passengers had to book ahead if they wanted this express train to stop at Hooky. Special trains were also booked for days out: there were seaside trips to Wales, and the whole of Hooky school once visited Liverpool.

Here in Hooky...

Villagers and railway workers formed a brass band in 1886, which rehearsed at the brewery. It is still going.

Express passing Hook Norton Station

Hooky train times

1887	1902	1939–45	1951
Railway line opens. A monthly cattle market begins next to the station.	Five trains a day run to both Chipping Norton and Banbury.	The line is busy carrying soldiers and airmen to local bases, plus ironstone to make steel for the war effort.	The last passenger train runs, but freight trains continue.

The Railway Hotel was next to the station.

All aboard the Hooky Flyer!

The light-hearted cartoon below shows the Hooky to Chipping Norton train bursting with passengers up to all sorts of fun and games. The Hooky Flyer ran up to five times a day early in the 20th century. But in real life very few travellers used the route and it didn't make much money for the railway, which relied on payments for transporting iron ore.

CHIPPY to HOOKIE and back the same day; if you're lucky.

1958	1963	1965	1971
A landslide on the cutting blocks the line to Chipping Norton.	September sees rail enthusiasts crowd onto the last train to cross the viaduct.	The railway tracks are blown up and sold as scrap metal.	Part of the old railway line becomes a nature reserve. The tunnel is later bricked up.

29

Iron from the ground

Stinking smoke once hung in clouds over Hooky as giant ovens baked rocks that men had hacked from the ground using picks and metal bars.

Who?

Several different firms ran quarries at various times, employing local men and boys to dig and carry the stone.

What?

'Toppers' dug away the soil until they reached rock. Then they hacked it out and loaded it onto carts. It was a tough, dangerous job. At first, boys led horses that pulled the carts away. Later, a track and wagons were used.

Why?

The stone contained iron ore which was sent away to be heated until it melted and poured out to make steel.

How?

It was tough, dangerous work. Teams worked from 6am to 6pm. The stone was sent off as it was or loaded into huge kilns whose heat turned it to pieces that were easier to transport.

This was the site of Hooky's first ironstone quarry.

Where?

There were quarries around to the north, east and south of the village. Some are now farmland, others are housing estates. Major firm Brymbo put up kilns and built a row of cottages for workers on the Milcombe Road. The houses are still there.

Here in Hooky...

Quarrymen were paid by how much rock they dug – if rain or snow stopped the work, they got no pay.

Ironstone years

1889

Hook Norton Ironstone Partnership (HNIP) begins large-scale quarrying and digs a tunnel under the Banbury Road to get the rock to the station.

1898

Steel firm Brymbo sets up an ironstone works and two years later builds a narrow-gauge railway line to haul its stone to the kilns, replacing horses and carts.

1901

Work begins on new sites bought by the Earl of Dudley near the viaduct south of the village. It has its own kiln.

1903

HNIP goes bust and six years later Brymbo buys its quarries.

1914–18

World War One creates massive demand for ironstone. The kilns run 24 hours a day to burn 5,000 tons of ore a week, five times the pre-war figure.

1926

Brymbo closes its kilns as demand for iron ore drops and it stops all quarrying five years later.

1939–46

World War Two means Britain needs steel and, by February 1943, 82 men and boys are hard at work. The quarries fall silent again in 1946.

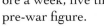

Vital for life

TITE LANE

This led to the tite at the bottom of Down End.

Fire and water play a big part in Hooky's history, from firefighting to digging for water.

The tite in Down End was obviously a place to meet up for a chat, too!

Here in Hooky...

In medieval times, grain was carted 2 miles to a water mill near Swerford for grinding into flour.

Water sources

- The Rop stream
- Two tites in Down End
- A tite at the foot of Middle Hill.
- A tite on common land on the south side of Hooky
- Washbrook ditch at Scotland End.

Boring buckets

Rich homes often had wells sunk in their gardens, but poorer villagers had no water supply in their houses. The children of Hook Norton must have got fed up with trekking out to fill buckets with water. They often collected it from the village tites, which were places where water collects naturally and were found at the locations listed to the left.

Firefighting in Hooky

1671	1731	1735	1896
All churches are ordered to store firefighting equipment. If the church bells ring unexpectedly, villagers rush to grab the buckets.	The church wardens buy a fire hook – a pole with metal prongs for removing roof thatch.	By now, the village has a fire cart. This year the church also spends 4 old pence to mend the fire buckets.	Hooky is one of the first villages in the area to have a volunteer fire brigade with its own fire engine, bought for £71.

Water problems

The Rop carried drainage water and waste, so it could be dirty and carry diseases such as typhoid. In 1936 officials were so concerned about typhoid that they started to cart in tanks of water from other villages. They soon worried also because the local water contains very little iodine, a natural mineral that helps our bodies to grow properly. Hooky finally got piped water in 1956, but it took another nine years for the village's sewage (toilet waste) to be treated properly.

Fire!

Wooden houses, thatched roofs and straw-filled barns burn easily, and for centuries people used candles for light and open fires for warmth, so fire was a constant risk.

This house on The Green was burned out in the early 1900s.

Villagers in fancy dress show off the fire cart. You can see it in St Peter's.

1896	1952	1995	2010
	The fire station opens, with a new fire engine stored inside. Four years later Hooky gets piped water.	Hooky firefighters are called out to a record 240 incidents in the village and the surrounding area.	Hooky wins a national award as fire station of the year for its fundraising.

Beer here!

BREWERY LANE

This leads to …
the brewery!

Hooky's brewery is famous because its beer is sold so widely, and today tourists visit the Victorian building where it is made.

Brewed on the farm

John Harris bought a farm in Hooky in 1849. Like some other farms at the time, it had a malt house where grain was soaked and then roasted to begin making beer.

Harris started brewing in 1856, and bought a shop that sold beer in Down End in 1859, purchasing the nearest pub to his brewery, the Pear Tree, ten years later. His business was so successful that he built a three-storey brewery in 1872, close to a good source of clean water. The brewery was employing 16 men and two boys in 1881.

Bigger and bigger

The brewery was rebuilt in 1899 into a larger structure with a steam engine to pump water and to power the machinery.

Workers stand proudly on the scaffolding as the new brewery is built.

Kids' work

Boys were employed to check machinery, and to help with deliveries. It took two horses to pull the heavy carts loaded with filled barrels up the hills that surround Hooky. A boy would sit with the driver and, when they reached the top, one horse was unhitched and the boy would walk the giant beast back to the brewery.

Brewing as seen by Hooky art teacher Joan Lawrence in 1972.

Horse power

Horse-pulled drays delivered the beer to local pubs and were joined by this steam wagon in 1904. The brewery stopped using horses in 1950, but started again in 1985 (see below).

◀ Today, Hook Norton Brewery still makes beer and is also a tourist attraction.

Here in Hooky...

John Harris's descendants, the Clarke family, still run the brewery.

Hooky at war

BRIDGE HILL

There was a prisoner-of-war camp near the top of Bridge Hill, behind the Sun Inn.

Many men and boys left Hooky to fight in World War One (1914–18), and some never returned. The war revived the ironstone quarries because the army and navy needed steel, and gave women a new role.

Suffering families

Twenty-seven Hooky-born men died in the war – about 10 per cent of the men of fighting age in the village. The dead included four sets of brothers, while Annie Robins lost both a son and a grandson. The youngest victim was 17-year-old Ernest Alfred Heritage, who seems to have lied about his age to sign up.

Red Cross fundraising

Villagers organised concerts to raise money for the Red Cross, set up in 1863 to save human life and health. It was very busy helping prisoners-of-war in World War One.

Helping horses

With the men away, women took on more paid work. The Women's Forage Corps helped the millions of horses that were vital to the British army.

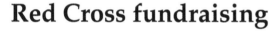

36

William Bloxham

William Bloxham was born in Hook Norton in 1885. He worked in the brewery office, but times were hard and, like many others, he emigrated to start a new life in Australia in 1912. Three years later he signed up as a soldier and twice returned to visit friends and family in Hooky before he was killed in France in 1917.

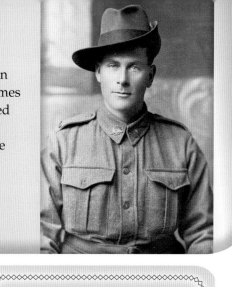

Glass to remember

A stained-glass window in St Peter's Church was created in memory of the Hook Norton men who died during World War One.

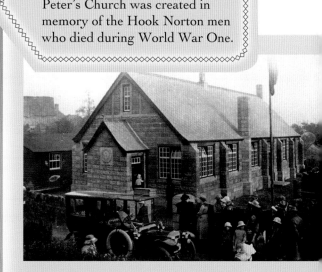

The Memorial Hall

The photograph above was taken at the opening of the Memorial Hall in 1922. It was built, at a cost of £2,500, in memory of those who had fought and worked in the war.

Here in Hooky...

In 1916 a shortage of men forced the brewery to take on women to work the machinery for the first time.

▶ This plaque in St Peter's lists those who died in World War One.

1914	✝	1918
CLAUDE ALLEN	ALBERT EMBRA	WILLIAM JAQUES
AUBREY ALLEN	ERNEST EMBRA	FREDERICK NASH
WILLIAM BEAVINGTON	ARTHUR GRANT	GEORGE PAINTIN
GEORGE BEAVINGTON	LAWRENCE GREY	JAMES PARGETER
WILLIAM BLOXHAM	ALFRED GIBBS	JOSEPH PINFOLD
WILLIAM BOLTON	DONALD HALL	ERNEST F. ROBINS
FRED BUSBY	ERNEST A. HERITAGE	E. JOHN ROBINS
M. FRED BUSBY	THOMAS HIATT	THOMAS ROSE · JNR ·
WALTER BUSBY	OLIVER HORN	ALBERT J. SIMMONS
GEORGE COLEMAN	THOMAS HONE	GEORGE SAVAGE
PERCY R. COOPER	RICHARD HYDE	FREDERICK TOWNLEY

"GREATER LOVE HATH NO MAN THAN THIS · THAT A MAN LAY DOWN HIS LIFE FOR HIS FRIENDS"

Plenty to enjoy

THE SHEARINGS T

Sheep were sheared, and the Flower Show was held, in the old Shearing Close.

In the years after World War One, Hooky's villagers found plenty to enjoy – especially on May Days and the yearly flower show.

May Day

This was a very old farming tradition to celebrate planting seeds in the fields. Children danced around the Maypole, and a girl was crowned May Queen. Victoria Page remembered it as a special occasion: 'On May Day, we used to starch our dresses so that they really stuck out!'

Street games

Children often played in the streets, as villager Phyllis Rathbone remembers: 'When it was really frosty we used to have a slide from the school to the Bell Inn… In the summer we used to play "whip the top" and marbles in the road.' When a horse-drawn cart went through the village, kids would climb up onto it for a ride, while their friends shouted out loud to make the horses go faster and make the journey bumpy!

Here in Hooky…

New houses with large gardens went up on The Bourne and Bourne Lane in the 1920s.

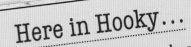

Flower Show

This annual summer event went way beyond showing off plants and produce. There were all sorts of fun and games.

Girls raced with hoops …

...while boys raced blindfold …

… or in sacks.

There were unusual football matches …

… and lots of dressing up!

Club Days

For years, self-help clubs had helped people save money to cover illness, hardship or funerals. Every May or June on Club Day they celebrated their work with stalls, games, races, music, food and drink (see left).

Got any gum, chum?

The commemorative march to remember past wars always starts on The Green.

World War Two (1939–45) saw Hooky welcome many evacuees and US troops, and everyday life changed.

Escaping London bombs

Children were sent to the countryside to escape the bombing. 130 children arrived in Hooky in 1939, and more followed later.

I am picking up wonderfully at HOOK NORTON.

Headmaster Arthur Miller, living next to the school, wrote the school log book through the War. ▼

◄ Cheerful postcards were made for evacuees to send home.

1939

4 September Opened school at 9am for evacuee children.

1940

19 June Wiring of school windows with half inch mesh and papering glass as precaution.

20 November Owing to two successive all night air raid alarms many children absent from school during morning sessions.

21 November Gardening class saw an English fighter plane (a Spitfire) chase a German plane.

1941

10 January First daylight air raid warning. Children took refuge under desks.

1943

9 March Allowed children to spend most of pm watching tanks etc pass by playground.

1944

2 July Opened Wesleyan [Methodist] school room and babies' class room to accommodate further evacuees. Brought large infant room into use as Rest Centre Canteen.

6 July Whole school now in use as Rest Centre.

17 July Number sleeping in Rest Centre down to 35 but not possible to open school.

Everyone had to keep their gas mask with them – children hung them on the backs of their chairs at school.

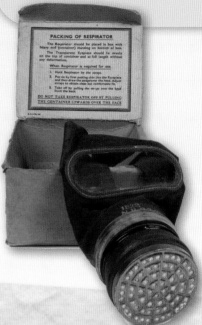

PACKING OF RESPIRATOR

Army visitors

American troops came to Hooky in 1943–44. The US Army separated its soldiers by skin colour: when off duty, white troops went to Chipping Norton while black ones came to Hooky. Children used to call out 'Got any gum, chum?' and would rush to the station when soldiers unloaded goods, hoping to be paid in coins or sweets for fetching sandwiches from the village.

Getting ready to fight

John Coppage saw how the local forces prepared to invade France in 1944:

'First, there were the low level flying aircraft… nearly touching the tops of the hedges and startling you and the animals. Second, the tank manoeuvres, all over the farm land, through hedges and over ditches…. Ammunition trains arrived continually… and droves of lorries took the boxes out to store in tents, all along the grass verges – we couldn't drive the tractor up to the fields.'

Dangerous munitions were stored in tents in fields so that if some exploded, the whole village wouldn't blow up.

Growing again

The 1970s and 80s saw new estates built on Rectory Road, Hollybush Road, Orchard Road, Chapel Street and Beanacre.

After World War Two, Hooky gained, and lost, a school, while the High Street changed.

New school

The school-leaving age was raised to 15 in 1947 and three years later Hook Norton Secondary Modern School opened. It had about 120 pupils, many coming in by bus from surrounding villages – sometimes they had to dig it out of the snow!

Meals on wheels

One teacher really stood out for pupil Chris Tobin: 'Mrs Bertha Collins used to ride a really old-fashioned lady's bike with several buckets hanging on the handlebars and she'd take all the old leftover food from the canteen for the pigs!'

Long warm-up

Footballers at Hooky secondary school had a long trek: 'When we played football we had to walk down to the Railway Hotel, to what used to be the old football field … by the time we got there we were just about jiggered! And then you had to walk all the way back!' (Pupil Tom Powell).

▲ The Beanacre housing estate was built near the site of an old quarry in 1986.

Here in Hooky...

Hooky had its own pottery from 1969, when Russell Collins started making honey pots.

The school was built with an open space in the middle.

Second becomes first

The secondary school closed in 1971, when Hook Norton primary school took over the buildings. Jane Orchard taught there: 'We loved having the classes on all four sides of the quadrangle, because you could see everyone – but you had to walk outside to go anywhere, whatever the weather. And the building was rather damp, so displays fell off the wall!'

Book shelves replaced desks when the old primary school became the village library.

The High Street changes again

Hooky's shops suffered as supermarkets in Banbury and Chipping Norton attracted customers in the 1980s and 1990s. Local businesses shut, including a bank, bakery and butcher – but the Williams family took over the village grocery shop in 1990 and still run it today.

The High Street lost its bank (above), but the village shop lives on (below).

Fair weather friends

Hooky is far from the sea but engineers at the Royal Navy's HMS Sultan base on the south coast visited for part of their training. In 1970 they used their skills to replace the weather vanes on top of St Peter's church tower.

Still changing

OLD SCHOOL END **T**

Old School End is where the school, its study centre and playing fields once stood.

In the 21st century villagers talk about broadband speeds as well as their broad beans!

A new school

Hook Norton primary moved to Sibford Road in 1993. The school was designed around a quad, like the old one – it's where the concrete hippos are today. Since then, solar panels have been fitted to the roof, new classrooms added, and the school extended in 2016 to fit in more pupils.

These days children still dance for May Day, but at the new school.

Changing land

Hooky continues to grow, with new estates bringing more people to live in the village.

Year	Estate	Number of houses	Previous use
1994	Old School End	33	Primary school
1995	Ironstone Hollow	27	Quarry, then farmland
2015	The Grange	37	Station, then a factory
2016	Bourne View	70	Farmland

Beat this

In 1997 Hooky rocked to its first music festival, called Folk in a Field. It moved to a larger site just outside the village in 2001, and was later renamed Music at the Crossroads. The annual event is now held in the village again.

◀ The sports and social club opened its club room alongside two football pitches, a cricket pitch, tennis courts and a Multi-Use Games Area (MUGA) in 2008.

Energy savers

In 2016 Hook Norton beat villages across Europe to win a prize for its renewable energy work. Hook Norton Low Carbon was set up in 2011 to help villagers with solar and wind power, sharing cars and electric bikes, and other projects to use energy efficiently and reduce our carbon footprint.

Three Bs again

Villagers still grow their own food in gardens and on allotments like these. Oh, and pigs are back in Hooky, reared by a group of villagers. So with the brewery and the village shop as well, Hooky still has its '3 Bs' !

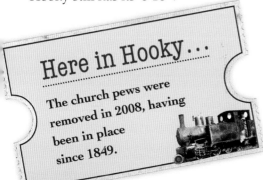

Here in Hooky...

The church pews were removed in 2008, having been in place since 1849.

Glossary and Index

Archaeologist: someone who studies human history by digging up the land.

Asylum: somewhere giving shelter and help to people in need.

Brewery: a place where beer is made.

Census: when the population is counted.

Churchwarden: someone in charge of non-religious jobs in a church.

Corbel: a stone sticking out from a wall to hold up a beam.

Cord: strands of thread.

Dray: a truck or cart for barrels.

Frontier: a border between countries or kingdoms.

Gargoyle: a spout to carry water off a building, carved to look like a face or animal.

Industry: making things, often with machinery.

Inscription: words written into stone.

Kiln: an oven for use in industry.

Manor: an area of land, often owned by a lord.

Massacre: violent killing of many people.

Medieval: the Middle Ages, roughly 500–1500.

Munitions: military weapons and stores.

Narrow-gauge: when railway tracks are closer together than usual.

Nonconformist: a Protestant who does not agree with the Anglican church.

Norman: a person from Normandy in France.

Pew: a long bench.

Quadrangle: a square space surrounded by buildings.

Quarry: a large pit where stone is dug out.

Tax: payment to the government or king.

Thatch: straw roof covering.

Typhoid: a dangerous illness that can kill.

Viaduct: a set of arches to carry a road or railway.

Will: a document saying what happens to your possessions after you die.

> **To find out more about Hooky:**
>
> Visit the Village Museum in the brewery Visitor Centre
>
> Look at the village history website: https://hook-norton.org.uk/history
>
> Follow the Village Trail: guide available from the website above.

Here in Hooky...

Sibford Road was known as The Horsefair until about 1900 because horses were traded there.

Acknowledgements

Author Sean Callery
Designer Sara Rafferty
Editor Donald Ratcliffe
Consultant Gill Geering
Photographer David McGill
Project manager Emma Callery
Printer KMS Litho, Hook Norton

This book was funded by a kind bequest from Betty Couldrey (pictured dressed as a Victorian, for fun), who lived in Hooky and died in 2016.

So many other people from Hook Norton have contributed directly to the making of this book that we can scarcely hope to mention them all. But they certainly include:
Alasdair Brown, Ian Buchanan, Pippa Cann, Richard Chalmers, James Clarke, Elaine Griggs, Pat Groome, Barbara Hicks, Hazel Hope, Jacqui Jones, Judi Leader, Tabby Lucas, Roy Meadow, Jane Orchard, Martin Quartermain, Gareth Richard, Bridget Shepherd, Barbara Summerell, James Tobin, Jackie White and, of course, all past and present members of the Hook Norton Local History Group.

About the author

Sean Callery has written more than 60 information and story books for children. He has lived in Hook Norton since 1990. Find out more on www.seancallery.co.uk.

Copyright details

Published by the Hook Norton Local History Group, 2017. ISBN 978-1-9998256-0-7

Copyright © Hook Norton Local History Group 2017

Picture credits